Learning About Fishes

By
DEBBIE ROUTH

COPYRIGHT © 2002 Mark Twain Media, Inc.

ISBN 1-58037-190-6

Printing No. CD-1536

Mark Twain Media, Inc., Publishers
Distributed by Carson-Dellosa Publishing Company, Inc.

Table of Contents

Introduction

Welcome to a series of books devoted to the *Chordata* phylum. A **chordate** is an animal that has a spinal cord. Most chordates have specialized body systems and paired appendages; all at some point in their lives have a notochord, dorsal nerve cord, and gill slits.

Every animal in the animal kingdom can be subdivided into two main groups. The **invertebrates** (without backbones) make up 95 percent of all the known animals. The **vertebrates** (with backbones) make up only five percent of the animal kingdom. The vertebrates, or chordates, are then divided even further into seven groups called classes—jawless fish, cartilaginous fish, bony fish, amphibians, reptiles, birds, and mammals. Each class has special characteristics all its own.

This book is devoted to the simplest **classes** (groups) of vertebrates called **fish**. Fish are vertebrates that live in various types of water. There are three main fish groups, and they are vastly different. Although the vertebrates in this group are very diverse, we can make a few generalizations that apply to all fish: they are vertebrates that breathe with gills, have scales, and swim with fins. The three classes of fish are **jawless fish**, **cartilaginous** (KART il AJ uh nus) **fish**, and **bony fish**. There are about as many **species** (kinds) of fish (about 20,000) as there are in all four of the other classes of vertebrates together.

Student observers will use many scientific process skills to discover the world of fish—their habits, behavior, and natural history. The reinforcement sheets that follow the lessons contain at least one higher-level thinking question.

So, student observers, put on those thinking caps, and use your process skills to observe, classify, analyze, debate, design, and report. This unit contains a variety of lessons that will help you practice scientific processes as you make exciting discoveries about these fascinating aquatic creatures called fish.

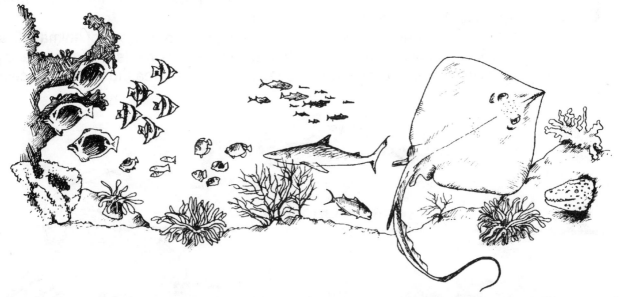

* **Teacher Note:** Each lesson opens with a manageable amount of text for the student to read. The succeeding pages contain exercises and illustrations that are varied and plentiful. Phonetic spellings and simple definitions for terms are also included to assist the student. The lessons may be used as a complete unit for the entire class or as supplemental material for the reluctant learner. The tone of the book is informal; a dialogue is established between the book and the student.

What Is a Fish?

Kingdom: *Animalia*
  Phylum: *Chordata*
    Subphylum: *Vertebrata*
      3 Classes: *Agnatha* (Ag NATH a) means "jawless fish"
                Chondrichthyes (Kon DRIK the eez) means "cartilaginous fish"
                Osteichthyes (OS tee IK the eez) means "bony fish"

Hello, student observers! Let's take to the water and learn about the simplest and oldest group of vertebrates in the animal kingdom. Fish live in most of the earth's bodies of water and have become a very successful and varied group of aquatic creatures. Fish are superbly designed for living underwater.

When you hear the word *fish,* what image forms in your mind? Some people visualize a streamlined bass; others visualize brightly-colored tropical fish that dart quickly in and out of coral reefs. To some people the word *fish* conjures up terrifying images of sharks, or they mistakenly visualize whales or dolphins. Together throughout this unit we will try to gain an understanding of the term *fish.*

Although the species of fish are vastly different, we can make a few generalizations that apply to all fish. **Fish** are ectothermic vertebrates that have scales and swim with fins. An **ectotherm** is an animal that is cold-blooded. A cold-blooded animal's body temperature changes with the temperature of its surroundings. Fish are **well-adapted** (suited) to all aquatic habitats. Since most fish live in water, they breathe by filtering the oxygen from the water as it flows over their gills. **Gills** are feathery organs that have many blood vessels. The dissolved oxygen passes from the water into the blood in the gills. The bloodstream carries the oxygen to all parts of the fish's body. Carbon dioxide, a waste product made by the fish, passes out of the bloodstream into the gills where it is removed from the body.

The term *fish* is used to describe three very different groups or classes of animals. The three main classes of fish are **jawless fish**, **cartilaginous fish**, and **bony fish**. These amazing animals have been extremely successful from the shallow surface areas to the deep ocean depths.

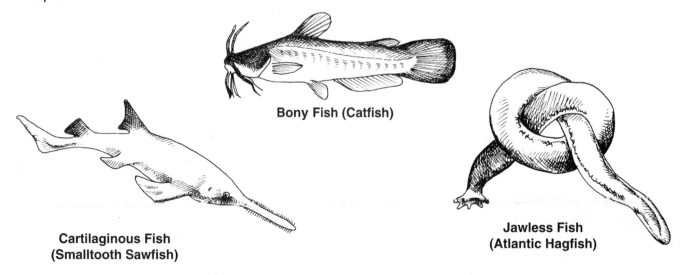

Bony Fish (Catfish)

**Cartilaginous Fish
(Smalltooth Sawfish)**

**Jawless Fish
(Atlantic Hagfish)**

Name:_____ Date: _____

What Is a Fish?: *Reinforcement Activity*

To the student observer: Do you know what organ fish use for breathing?

_____

Analyze: What would happen to the body temperature of a fish if the water temperature dropped?

_____

_____

Directions: Complete the questions below.

1. Fish are the oldest and _____ vertebrates.

2. Fish are _____ or cold-blooded vertebrates.

3. A cold-blooded animal's body temperature _____ with the temperature of its surroundings.

4. List four main characteristics of fish.

    a. _____

    b. _____

    c. _____

    d. _____

5. What are the three main classes of fish?

    a. _____

    b. _____

    c. _____

What Are Vertebrates?

Kingdom: *Animalia*
   Phylum: *Chordata* (kor DAT uh) means "having a cord"
     Subphylum: *Vertebrata* (vert a BRAT uh) means "having vertebrae"

Chordates

Animals are divided into two groups—invertebrates and vertebrates. **Invertebrates** are animals that have no backbone or spine, such as worms, insects, spiders, jellyfish, and many other sea animals. **Vertebrates** are a subphylum of the *chordata* phylum. The earliest known vertebrate was a fishlike animal, **ostracoderm** (as TRAK uh durm). A **chordate** is any animal that has a notochord (NOHT uh kord) inside it at some point in its development. A **notochord** is a stiff, rodlike structure that can bend. It offers support to the organism. The notochord is located just beneath the nerve cord. Besides a notochord, all chordates have a hollow nerve cord that runs down the animal's back. All chordates at some point in their lives have paired gill slits. In fish, the gill slits become gills; however, in other animals, the gill slits disappear. Chordates have **bilateral symmetry**, which means they have matching right and left sides. Fish, frogs, snakes, birds, and elephants are all animals classified in the phylum *chordata*.

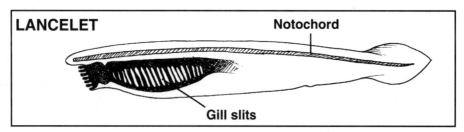

Vertebrates

Vertebrates have small bones or a tough fiber called **cartilage** that replaces the notochord. These animals have little pieces of backbone called **vertebrae** (VERT uh bray). All vertebrates have an **endoskeleton** (an inner skeleton); a backbone; eyes, nostrils, and a mouth on their heads; and usually two pairs of limbs. An endoskeleton protects the inside organs and gives support. The vertebrates have been divided into seven classes: three classes of fish, amphibians, reptiles, birds, and mammals. Each class is more complex than the one before it. The last class, mammals, is the most complex of all. Mammals include a highly-organized animal called man.

Vertebrates Run Hot and Cold

One important difference in vertebrates is the ability to regulate body temperature. Animals produce heat as they break down the food they eat. Some animals lose the body heat created by the digestion of food as fast as they produce it. These animals are **ectotherms** (cold-blooded), which means the temperature of their surroundings regulates their body temperature. Fish, amphibians, and reptiles are ectothermic animals. Animals that can control the loss of body heat and maintain their temperature with internal processes are **endotherms** (warm-blooded). Birds and mammals are endothermic animals. You are an endothermic animal. Your body temperature stays the same no matter how warm or cold it gets outside.

Name:_____ Date: _____

What Are Vertebrates?: *Reinforcement Activity*

To the student observer: Do you know what organ the skull protects?

_____

Analyze: Based on what you know, what process converts food into energy?

_____

Directions: Answer the following questions to review the main concepts.

1. What are three main characteristics shared by all chordates at some point in their development?

   a. _____

   b. _____

   c. _____

2. Animals are divided into two groups. Can you identify and explain them?

   a. _____

   _____

   b. _____

   _____

3. What are the two groups of vertebrates based on their ability to regulate their body temperature? Explain the difference.

   a. _____

   _____

   _____

   b. _____

   _____

   _____

Name:_____ Date: _____

Vertebrates: *Crossword Puzzle*

To the student observer: Prove how much you know about vertebrates by completing the crossword below.

ACROSS

1. Frogs and toads
7. The most complex animal
8. An animal with a backbone
10. Little pieces of bone
12. A tough fiber, more flexible than bone
14. A skeleton protects your _____.
16. Vertebrates usually have four _____.
17. All chordates have a _____ nerve cord.
19. A skeleton on the inside
20. Cold-blooded vertebrates

DOWN

2. This means that vertebrates have matching right and left sides. (two words)
3. A limbless reptile
4. Means "having vertebrae"
5. Means "having a cord"
6. Class a turtle belongs to
9. A vertebrate with feathers
11. Man, cats, and dogs
13. Make up three classes of vertebrates
15. Warm-blooded vertebrates
18. A stiff rod of cartilage

Observers: What do each of the animals on this page have in common? _____

_____

Ichthyology

Ichthyology (IK thee AL uh jee) is the study of fish. **Ichthyologists** study fishes' ancestors, anatomy, feeding habits, reproduction methods, migratory patterns, parenting, predator/prey relationships, and their environment. An ichthyologist may be a specialist who studies sharks or monsters of the abyss. Or he or she may be a park ranger who monitors recreation areas for fishermen. An ichthyologist may be someone like you who sets up his or her first aquarium tank for pleasure.

Fish have outdone all the other animals in terms of variety and colors. They are an important animal to man; many people around the world depend on fish for their main source of protein. Fish have also given man a favorite hobby, fishing. Many people enjoy the challenge of the catch. Fish populations are constantly monitored to determine if overfished species are regaining their numbers. Fish make excellent bioindicators because they are very sensitive to chemicals in the water. A **bioindicator** is any organism whose health reflects the health of the ecosystem. Healthy waters mean healthy fish. Ichthyologists study fish because fish reflect the health of our planet.

Other people enjoy keeping fish in captivity. Pet stores and technology have made available many interesting and elaborate homes for captive fish. Even the landscaping of many homes today incorporates a goldfish pond with aquatic plants. As you can see, ichthyology is a wide-open field. Are you an ichthyologist? Do you go fishing or have an aquarium?

The History of Fish

Ichthyology—The Study of Fish

Fish are the most ancient of the **vertebrates** (animals with backbones). The early fish had no jaws, fins, or scales, but they did have a backbone, which set them apart from the **invertebrates** (animals without a backbone). Most scientists agree that fish developed from soft-bodied, filter-feeding **organisms** (living things) similar to the lancelets of today. Today there are over 20,000 species of fish. They have adapted well and have amazing variety. Some fish live out of water, others fly, and some even walk on their fins.

Fossils

Fish skeletons fossilized well, telling us about an extinct fish that lived long ago.

The Steps From Fish to Fossil
- The dead fish sinks to the bottom of the lake.
- The scarcity of scavengers allows sediment to cover the body of the fish, leaving it intact.
- Years later, the lake is gone, and its bottom layers have formed layers of sandstone.
- The sandstone is lifted by the earth's own movements.
- Erosion uncovers the fish fossil.
- The imprint of the fish's body is hardened into the clay.
- Minerals have turned its bones to stone.

Ostracoderms and Other Early Fish

What is known about early fish comes from fossil records. One of the earliest fish was the **ostracoderm**, a jawless fish with heavy bony plates. Fossils of these early fish were usually found where ancient streams emptied into the sea. We do not know for certain if these early fish were freshwater fish or **marine** (saltwater) fish. This early type, the ostracoderm, is considered to be the first fish. It moved slowly, scavenging for food on the muddy bottom. The fossil evidence indicates that primitive fish developed rigid skeletons, paired fins, and the greatest advance of all—jaws. The movable jaws enabled fish to bite and chew. Most fish today have movable jaws and paired fins, except for the lamprey and hagfish. Other early fish were the **acanthodian**, **holostean**, and **teleost**. These early fish developed useful fins that gave them stability.

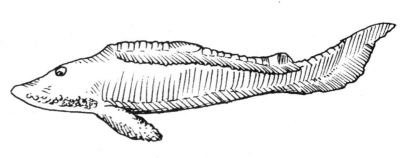

Famous Fish

There are fish alive today that tell us about the past. These "living fossils," the **coelacanths** (SEE luh kanths), surprised scientists when they were discovered in 1938 in South Africa. They were thought to be extinct. The living coelacanth is almost identical to the fossils.

Name:_____ Date: _____

The History of Fish: *Reinforcement Activity*

To the student observer: Do you know which fish is considered to be the first fish?

_____

Analyze: Why was the hinged jaw an important milestone for fish? _____

_____

Directions: Answer the following questions.

1. What three fish traits did the early fish lack? _____

_____

_____

2. How do scientists learn about fish that lived in ancient times? _____

_____

_____

3. What fish that is alive today is considered a "living fossil"? Why is it called a "living fossil"?

_____

_____

_____

4. Sequence the seven steps of fossilization.

    _____ a. A fish dies and sinks to the bottom.

    _____ b. Minerals have turned its bones to stone.

    _____ c. The body doesn't decompose; sediment covers the body, leaving it intact.

    _____ d. Erosion uncovers the fish.

    _____ e. Years later, the lake is gone, and layers of sandstone have formed.

    _____ f. Earth's movements move the sandstone layers.

    _____ g. An imprint of the fish's body is hardened into the clay.

Built for Underwater Life: *External Anatomy*

Fins

Most fish have a streamlined shape and compact body that is ideal for moving underwater. Most fish have a narrow, pointed snout that helps them cut through the water. The **caudal fin** is used to propel the fish forward. The **dorsal and anal fins** act as stabilizers, which help to keep the fish from rolling over onto its side. A fish's paired **pectoral** and **pelvic fins** help to hold the fish steady and aid it in maneuvering. They are also used as brakes when the fish needs to stop.

Scales

Fish are covered by a protective transparent skin, which produces a lubricating **mucous**. This helps the fish move through the water. Most fish have one of four kinds of plates called **scales**, which form an outer skeleton. The scaly, colorful armor overlaps and forms a shield against injury. Fish continue to grow their entire lives, and their scales grow with them. You can calculate the age of a fish by counting the growth rings that form as the scales expand.

The four main types of scales are **cycloid**, **ctenoid**, **placoid**, and **ganoid**. The most common scales are the ctenoid and cycloid, which are found on true bony fish. Ctenoid scales have teeth along the edge and are rough to the touch. These are found on fish such as bass, bluegill, and perch. Cycloid scales have a smooth surface and are found on carp and salmon. Placoid scales are found on cartilaginous fish such as sharks and rays. They look like tiny teeth or thorns and feel like rough sandpaper. The fourth type of scale, ganoid, is found on primitive fish such as the gar. Ganoid scales are hard, interlocking, and diamond-shaped.

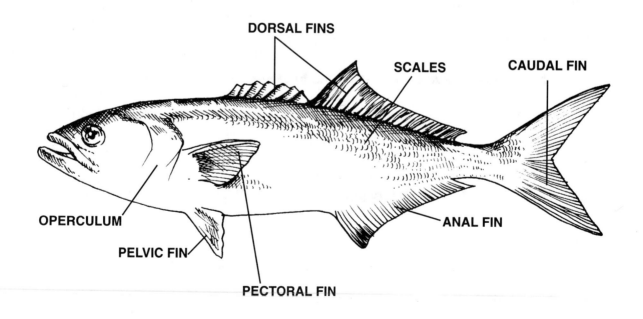

Name:_____ Date: _____

External Anatomy: *Reinforcement Activity*

To the student observer: Can you describe how a fish's body is built for underwater life?

_____

_____

Analyze: What advantage does the shape of its body and head have for a fish trying to move in its habitat?

_____

_____

Directions: Answer the following questions.

1. Identify and give the purpose of the four kinds of fins.

   a. Fin _____ purpose _____

   b. Fin _____ purpose _____

   c. Fin _____ purpose _____

   d. Fin _____ purpose _____

2. Identify the four kinds of scales and the corresponding group of fish for each kind.

   a. Scale _____ fish _____

   b. Scale _____ fish _____

   c. Scale _____ fish _____

   d. Scale _____ fish _____

3. What is the purpose of a fish's scales? _____

   _____

4. Identify the type of scale for each description.

   _____ a. interlocking and diamond-shaped; found on gar

   _____ b. have teeth and are rough to the touch; found on bony fish

   _____ c. have a smooth surface; found on bony fish

   _____ d. look like tiny teeth and feel like sandpaper; found on sharks

Built for Underwater Life: *Internal Anatomy*

Buoyancy

Most fish float because of a special feature called a **swim bladder**. The swim bladder is a thin-walled sac that can inflate or deflate when the gases from the blood pass into or out of it. This helps the fish move up and down in the water or remain at a particular depth. As the swim bladder fills with gas, it becomes buoyant and rises. As the swim bladder deflates, the fish sinks because it becomes less buoyant. Sharks do not have a swim bladder, but they do have a large liver that produces oil, which is less dense than water. This provides some buoyancy. Constant swimming and lift from the flow of water over a shark's lateral fins also help prevent it from sinking.

Senses

Fish have all five senses that we have and one more—a true sixth sense. Fish have limited vision of about 100 feet. Some fish have keen senses of smell that help them locate prey. The shark has a very keen sense of smell and can detect blood one-half kilometer away. Some fish have receptors on their heads that help them navigate using the earth's magnetic field. The sense of touch is conveyed to fish by nerve organs scattered over the skin; fish even detect physical pain. Most fish have an extraordinary sixth sense that is able to detect movement and currents in the water. Sensory organs called the **lateral line system** alert fish to the movement of other organisms around them.

Breathing

Fish use their **gills** to obtain oxygen and give off carbon dioxide. An outer covering called the **operculum** (oh PUR kyoo lum) protects the feathery gills. Water passes over the gills from front to back and provides a constant source of oxygen. The efficiency of this type of respiration allows fish to have a single-loop circulatory system with a two-chambered heart.

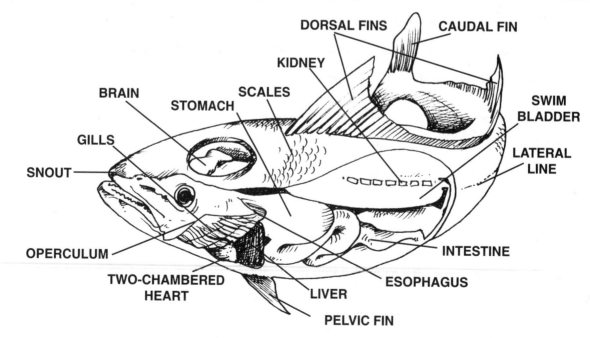

Name:_____ Date: _____

Internal Anatomy: *Reinforcement Activity*

To the student observer: Can you describe how a fish's internal body is adapted for underwater life?

_____

_____

_____

Analyze: Besides breathing, what other challenges would a fish have in trying to live on land?

_____

_____

Directions: Answer the questions below.

1. How do fish float? (Be specific.) _____

    _____

    _____

    _____

2. Why are sharks less buoyant than other fish? _____

    _____

3. What fish have the keenest sense of smell? _____

4. What is the lateral line system, and what does it do? _____

    _____

    _____

    _____

5. Why do fish function so well with a single-loop circulatory system and a two-chambered heart?

    _____

    _____

    _____

6. Why are fish able to function so well with limited eyesight? _____

    _____

    _____

Name:_____ Date: _____

Internal and External Anatomy: *Reinforcement Activity*

To the student observer: Can you interpret a diagram of a fish?

Directions: Use the diagram to complete the following questions.

1.   Label the diagram using the word bank below.

swim bladder	dorsal fins	pelvic fin	gills	caudal fin
lateral line	snout	operculum	scales	brain

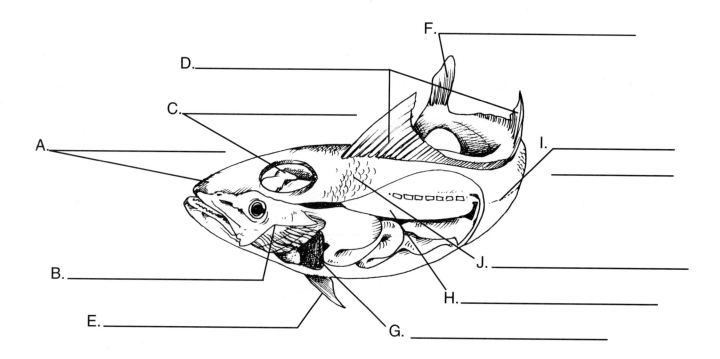

2.   What does Part B protect? _____

3.   What is the function of the snout, caudal, dorsal, and pectoral fins? _____

_____

4.   What does the fish use Part G for? _____

_____

5.   What does the fish use Part I for? _____

_____

6.   What part helps with buoyancy? _____

14

What Is Classification?

To classify means to put into groups based on a trait or characteristic that is unique to whatever you are classifying. **Classification** is a way of organizing things or information. Music is classified as rock, easy listening, classical, country, jazz, etc. This makes finding the kind of music you like easier when you go shopping for a new CD. The CDs are then classified even further, according to the artist who produced the CD. Many things are classified in our lives. The library, the grocery store, and your own kitchen are classified. Your dresser may be classified so you can get dressed quickly in the morning.

Scientists found that classifying all living things made it easier to learn and study about them. It helps avoid errors in communication among scientists throughout the world. Classification also makes it easier for scientists to identify newly-discovered organisms. Scientists who classify living things are called **taxonomists**. **Taxonomy** (taks ON uh mee) is the science of classification.

Traits

Traits are used to help taxonomists group organisms. A **trait** is a characteristic that helps us identify living things. For example, all birds have feathers, and all giraffes have long necks. Organisms within a group may share certain traits; however, no two are exactly the same. They each have their own individual differences. We call these **individual traits**. All birds have feathers, but some birds have different kinds of feathers. Some giraffes have longer necks than others. All humans have certain traits; yet no two humans are exactly the same—not even identical twins. There are always individual differences. These individual differences help us recognize different members of the same group. Think of your friends and family; you know one another by such individual traits as size, hair type, skin tones, or the shape of the face. Can you think of traits common to all human beings? What are some traits common to all fish?

Goosefish

Pancake Batfish

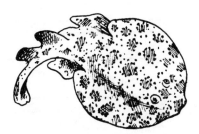

Lesser Electric Ray

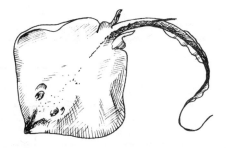

Atlantic Stingray

15

Name:_____ Date: _____

Classification: *Reinforcement Activity*

To the student observer: Humans and fish are alike in some ways. They share certain traits that place them both in the same group. For example, humans and fish are living things because they are made up of cells and carry out life processes. They are both animals because they move about in search of food. They are both vertebrates because they have backbones.

Human Trait or Fish Trait?: Identifying Organisms by Group Traits

Directions: Study the traits below and decide if the trait belongs to a fish or a human, based on their individual differences. Place an "X" in the correct column.

Traits	Human	Fish
1. Some hair covering		
2. Some scale covering		
3. Females nurse their young.		
4. Give birth to live young		
5. Live on land		
6. Breathe by gills		
7. Have fins		
8. Lay eggs		
9. Breathe through lungs		
10. Walk on two legs		
11. Have a swim bladder		
12. Embryos develop outside the female's body.		

13. Do all humans have the traits you listed as human? _____

14. The traits you have identified are _____ traits.

15. Are all fish exactly alike? _____

Why or why not? _____

_____

_____

_____

Classification of Fish

Kingdom: *Animalia*
   Phylum: *Chordata*
      Subphylum: *Vertebrata*
         Class: *Agnatha* (jawless fish)
              Chondrichthyes (cartilaginous fish)
              Osteichthyes (bony fish)

Fish, like all living things, are **classified** (placed into groups), which makes it easier to learn about them. Classification is based on common ancestors in the same way you are related to your family members.

Scientists have identified over 20,000 species of fish; however, it is difficult to keep track of so many species. To ease their burden, taxonomists have divided all the known species of fish into one of three **classes** (groups). Taxonomists do not group organisms simply because they look alike. They study their cells, the way they grow and develop, their blood, and even their internal and external body structures before deciding to which group they belong.

Three Classes of Fish

Osteichthyes - the largest and most varied group; the bony fish
    Examples: catfish, bass, trout, and bluegill.

Chondrichthyes - the fish with cartilage skeletons
    Examples: sharks, rays, and skates

Agnatha - the smallest and oldest group; the jawless fish
    Examples: hagfish and lamprey

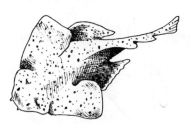

Chondrichthyes
Cartilaginous Fish
(Pacific Angel Shark)

Osteichthyes
Bony Fish
(Trout)

Agnatha
Jawless Fish
(Sea Lamprey)

Fish World Diversity: *Types of Fish*

Approximately 70 percent of the earth's surface is covered with water. Most of this water is in the oceans and seas. More fish live in the oceans of the world than in fresh water. The greatest varieties of fish inhabit tropical waters. The modern fish of today are classified into three classes. The simplest fish are the **jawless fish**, class *agnatha.* These fish have cartilage skeletons and lack a hinged jaw. They closely resemble the ancient fish of the past. The second group is the **cartilaginous fish**, class *chondrichthyes.* Fish in this group have skeletons made of cartilage. **Cartilage** is a tough, flexible tissue that is not as rigid as bone. The third group is the largest group, the bony fish. **Bony fish**, class *osteichthyes,* have skeletons made of bone. You are probably most familiar with these fish.

Class Agnatha: Jawless Fish

The jawless fish are the simplest and oldest vertebrates. These fish are scavengers or parasites that feed off the flesh and fluids of other fish. Jawless fish look very different from most fish. They have round mouths and are long and snakelike in shape. Jawless fish have a flexible cartilage skeleton and slimy skin without scales. Cartilage tissue is not as rigid as bone. For instance, you have cartilage in the tip of your nose and your ears. Lamprey and hagfish are the only jawless fish. Lampreys live in fresh water, and hagfish live in the sea.

Lamprey lay huge numbers of eggs in nests made of stones. The eggs hatch into blind burrowing larvae that live in mud and filter food from it for seven years. At seven years, the larvae undergo **metamorphosis**, a change in form. After metamorphosis, the lamprey has changed into its adult form with a sucker-shaped mouth and eyes that allow it to see. The lamprey attaches itself to a host fish and sucks its blood. It has an anticoagulant in its saliva that keeps the victim's blood from clotting.

Hagfish are scavengers who live only in **marine** (saltwater) environments. They move slowly in the cold water, using sensory tentacles to locate dead or dying fish. They often form an attachment to a host fish and feed until it is a hollow shell.

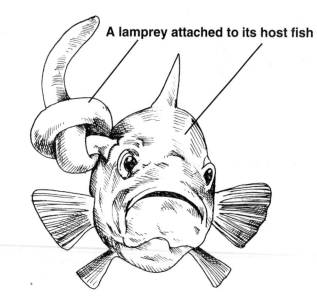
A lamprey attached to its host fish

Detail of a lamprey's sucker-shaped mouth

Fish World Diversity: *Types of Fish (cont.)*

Class Chondrichthyes: Cartilaginous Fish

The cartilaginous fish include sharks, rays, and skates. These fish have skeletons made of cartilage. The cartilage skeleton may be an adaptation for deep-sea life. They are among the most primitive of the large animals of today. Unlike the jawless fish, they do have a hinged jaw, paired fins, and scales. The scales of sharks are like rough teeth, causing their skins to feel like sandpaper. If you rub a shark from front to back, they feel smooth, but if you rub the opposite way, the feeling is painful. Sharks have torpedo-shaped bodies, and their muscles are attached to their skins instead of to their skeletons. Like most animals, many sharks eat other organisms for food. Their jaws are very powerful—the force is estimated at 20 tons per square inch for an eight-foot shark. The jaw is not bound to the brain case, allowing the jaws to protrude during attack. Its deadly teeth equally match the strength of the shark's jaw. Its teeth are matched to the type of prey it eats. Sharks do not have to worry about losing a tooth; they seem to have an endless supply. If a tooth is lost or damaged, a new one quickly moves into place. Not all sharks are meat-eaters, however. The whale shark, the largest of all fish, is a harmless plant-eater. Very few sharks are dangerous to man. Out of the hundreds of species, perhaps a dozen have been known to attack without reason. Most attacks occur when humans invade sharks' natural habitats.

Rays and skates are close relatives of the sharks. They have wing-like pectoral fins running the length of the head and body and gill slits underneath them. Most rays and skates live on the seabed; they feed on fish, shellfish, and worms. Some have poison spines on their backs or tails, so they can defend themselves. Scientists classify the rays and skates as kite-like sharks.

Fish World Diversity: *Types of Fish (cont.)*

Class Osteichthyes: Bony Fish

The most numerous and varied group are the bony fish. Bony fish have skeletons made of both bone and cartilage. These include familiar fish such as perch, bass, catfish, and gold-fish. Bony fish have hinged jaws, paired fins, hard protective scales, and covered gills. The **operculum**, a half circle just beneath the fish's eye, covers and protects the gills. The gill coverings clamp shut as the fish takes in a mouthful of water. Then they flap open as the water is pushed out the gills.

Bony fish have a unique sense—a cross between seeing and hearing just beneath their skin. A row of tiny, visible holes connects to a canal, called the **lateral line**, that is filled with sensitive nerves. The lateral line alerts the fish to changes in the flow of water. A goldfish uses the lateral line to keep it from bumping into the transparent glass walls of its aquarium.

Bony fish also have another unique adaptation called a **swim bladder**. By changing the amount of gas in this sac above the stomach, the fish are able to stay floating at certain depths. To rise in the water, they fill the swim bladder with air; to lower themselves, they release gas from the sac. They can then maintain a certain depth without moving a single muscle.

The bony fish are divided into three groups: the lobe-finned fishes, lungfishes, and ray-finned fishes. The modern coelacanth is a type of lobe-finned fish. The lungfish has lungs as well as gills. It can survive when rivers dry up or have low levels of oxygen. There are only a few surviving species of lungfish. The third group, the ray-finned fish, is the largest group of bony fishes. They have adapted to every kind of aquatic habitat. They have fanlike fins made of bony rays. Salmon, guppies, tuna, seahorses, and clown trigger fish belong to this group.

Name:_____ Date: _____

Fish World Diversity: *Reinforcement Activity*

To the student observer: Where do most fish live? _____

_____

Analyze: Why do you think the bony fish have more special traits than the other fish groups?

_____

_____

1. List the three groups of fish in order from simplest to the most complex and give an example of each.

   a. Group _____ Example _____

   b. Group _____ Example _____

   c. Group _____ Example _____

2. Identify and describe the oldest and simplest class. _____

_____

_____

3. Identify and describe the largest class. _____

_____

_____

4. Which class of fish has scales, paired fins, and a skeleton made of cartilage?

_____

5. Which group lives as parasites and scavengers?

_____

Name:_____ Date: _____

Name That Shark!: *Classification Activity*

All organisms are given a scientific name. Each organism is given a specific name because there are often too many common names for things. Even in the same language, there are sometimes several words to describe the same object. An international system for naming organisms is necessary so scientists can avoid errors in communication. The system by which all organisms are named is called **binomial nomenclature**. It was developed by Carolus Linnaeus. This system is based on the Latin language. The meanings of words in Latin do not change because it is an unspoken language today. Binomial nomenclature is a two-name naming system that consists of a genus name and a species name. The genus name comes first followed by the species name. The genus is capitalized, and the species is not. Both names are italicized. There are seven levels of classification—kingdom, phylum or division, class, order, family, genus, and species. Each level has a Latin name to describe the group.

Level	Latin name
Kingdom:	Animalia
Phylum:	Chordata
Class:	Chondrichthyes
Order:	Lamniformes
Family:	Sphyrnidae
Genus:	*Sphyrna*
Species:	*lewini*

1. To which kingdom does the shark belong? _____

2. The shark is a member of which class? _____

3. To which phylum does the shark belong? _____

4. All hammerhead sharks belong to the family _____.

5. What is the scientific name of the hammerhead shark above? _____

6. What language is binomial nomenclature based on? _____

7. Why do organisms need a scientific name? _____

    _____

    _____

8. Who developed the two-name naming system we use today? _____

Identifying Shark Families: *Using a Dichotomous Key*

Some people enjoy identifying organisms as a hobby. Bird-watchers enjoy identifying birds in their area. Some people like to try to name trees. By using a dichotomous (dy KAH toh mus) key and examining the leaves, you can usually identify the tree. A **dichotomous key** is a tool used by taxonomists to identify organisms. It lists two contrasting observable traits that you can easily recognize. By picking the correct option that matches your organism, you can narrow it down by its features until you can identify it. Dichotomous keys are often found in field guides. Use the pairs of traits on page 24 to identify which family each of the sharks on page 25 belongs to.

To the student observer: You will use this investigation to identify the shark families. Use the figure below as a guide to identify the parts of the shark used in the key. Remember, classification is a method of separating closely-related organisms into smaller groups. The key is arranged in steps with two descriptive statements at each step.

Procedure: Read sentences 1A and 1B of the key. You must <u>always</u> begin with a choice from the first pair of descriptions. At the end of the description, there is either the family name or directions to go on to another step. If you use the key correctly, you will discover the correct family name for each shark species.

Continue processing the pairs of descriptive traits until each shark has been identified. Write the family name on the line below each shark on page 25.

A TYPICAL SHARK

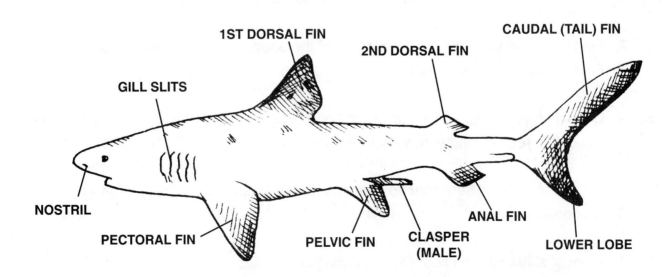

Identifying Shark Families: *Using a Dichotomous Key (cont.)*

Shark Families Dichotomous Key

1. A. Body kite-like .... Go to 10
   B. Body not kite-like .... Go to 2

2. A. No pelvic fin and nose saw-like .... Family Pristiophoridae
   B. Pelvic fin present .... Go to 3

3. A. Six gill slits present .... Family Hexanchidae
   B. Five gill slits present .... Go to 4

4. A. Only one dorsal fin .... Family Scyliorhinidae
   B. Two dorsal fins .... Go to 5

5. A. Mouth at front of snout .... Family Rhincodontidae
   B. Mouth on underside of head .... Go to 6

6. A. Head expanded on side with eyes at end of expansion .... Family Sphyrnidae
   B. Head not expanded .... Go to 7

7. A. Top and bottom half of caudal fin exactly the same .... Family Isuridae
   B. Top half of caudal fin different from bottom half .... Go to 8

8. A. First dorsal fin very long, half the length of the body .... Family Pseudotriakidae
   B. First dorsal fin regular length .... Go to 9

9. A. Caudal fin very long, as long as entire body .... Family Alopiidae
   B. Caudal fin regular length, nose needle-like .... Family Scapanorhynchidae

10. A. Small dorsal fin present near tip of tail .... Family Rajidae
    B. No dorsal fin present near tip of tail .... Go to 11

11. A. Front of shark has two horn-like appendages .... Family Mobulidae
    B. No horn-like appendages .... Family Dasyatidae

Name:_____ Date: _____

Identifying Shark Families: *Using a Dichotomous Key (cont.)*

Directions: Identify each shark family using the dichotomous key on page 24.

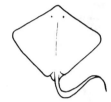

A. _____

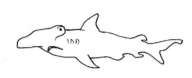

B. _____

C. _____

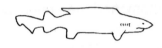

D. _____

E. _____

F. _____

G. _____

H. _____

I. _____

J. _____

K. _____

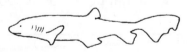

L. _____

Name:_____ Date: _____

Simulating Buoyancy: *Student Lab*

To the student observer: Most bony fish have an internal organ called the swim bladder. This organ is a gas-filled sac that lies at the top of the body cavity above the stomach and near the backbone. The swim bladder allows the fish to float.

Problem: How does the swim bladder work?

Materials: Two small balloons
Bucket or sink filled with water
Clamps to close balloons
Paper clip
6–8 metal keys

Procedure:
1. Fill the bucket or sink three-fourths full of water.
2. Blow up one balloon fully. Fasten the balloon with a small clamp.
3. Submerge the balloon in the water by pushing it down to the bottom, and then release it. What happens?
4. Blow up a second balloon slightly with only a small amount of air, and fasten it securely.
5. Submerge it as you did in Step 3.
6. Remove the balloon from the water, and blow a little more air into the balloon, and then fasten it again. Submerge again as you did in Step 3, and observe what happens. (Repeat this step several times until the balloon is fully inflated.)
7. Tie 6–8 keys together with a paper clip, and drop them into the water. What happens?
8. Attach the paper clip of keys to the clamp on the fully-inflated balloon. Hang the keys as close to the balloon as possible. Drop the objects into the water.
9. Using a clamp, add or release air until the balloon floats just under the surface of the water as shown in the figure above.

Observations:

1. What happened after you released the fully-inflated submerged balloon? _____

_____

_____

2. What happened after you released the slightly-inflated balloon? _____

_____

_____

3. What did you observe as you gradually added more air and submerged the balloon?

_____

_____

_____

Name:_____ Date: _____

Simulating Buoyancy: *Student Lab (cont.)*

Analyzing Results and Drawing Conclusions:

1. What relationship exits between the amount of air in a balloon and its ability to float?

   _____

   _____

   _____

2. Where is the swim bladder located? Describe its size. _____

   _____

   _____

3. What do you think happens to the swim bladder as it fills with gases? Does this do anything for the fish?

   _____

   _____

   _____

4. What do you think happens to the swim bladder when it releases gases? Does this do anything for the fish?

   _____

   _____

   _____

5. Where do you think the gases come from? _____

   _____

6. Think about the balloon and the keys. What does the balloon represent? What do the keys represent?

   _____

   _____

7. How does this demonstration explain how a fish can remain in the same spot just below the surface?

   _____

   _____

   _____

Fish World: *Where Do Fish Swim?*

Fish live in all types of habitats, but they only live in two kinds of water. Freshwater species live and swim in only fresh water. The other kind of water is where most fish live, marine (salt) water. Some fish could make up a third group; some fish live where salt water and fresh water meet. This is called brackish water. These fish live in estuaries. Only a small part of all the water on Earth is fresh water. We must take care of this small amount of water because many organisms need fresh water to survive. It would seem that fish are free to travel about in lakes and rivers. However, most are restricted to certain areas to which they have adapted. The water temperature and type of food are examples of limiting factors that keep fish restricted to certain areas.

Fresh Water

The inland water contains only about one-third of all the known **species** (types) of fish. They live in various freshwater habitats. They live and swim in natural and man-made lakes, rivers, streams, and creeks. Each type of freshwater habitat has its own selection of plants and animals that depend on it. The action of ice sheets during the **ice age** or the movements of the earth's plates formed the natural lakes. Man developed the practice of building lakes to provide more sources of fresh water. They have made many freshwater reservoirs to meet the water needs of people in towns and cities. Some lakes are the result of draining rivers. Lakes have a great amount of nutrients flowing into them and are usually rich in plant and animal life. Areas high in acid content are usually the deep lakes, and they have limited plant and animal life. The plants and animals that live there need special adaptations to survive these nutrient-poor waters. Rivers and streams begin as ground water that gathers on high ground and forms a pathway to the sea. The headwaters are usually clear, cool waters that move swiftly over rocks. It is difficult for plants to get established in these waters, but mosses and liverworts line the banks. Animals survive by hiding in crevices or attaching themselves to rocks. Most of these animals must be filter feeders. The fast-moving waters bring the food to them. Trout do well in this habitat. As the stream slows down and the land begins to level out, the stream grows into a river. The gravel, silt, and sand are deposited as the water moves less rapidly. These deposits cause the rivers to twist and turn. Several types of fish can be found in this kind of habitat, such as pike, bass, and perch. Finally, the river crosses the flatlands and empties into the sea.

Estuaries

As the river meets the ocean, the river channel is flooded, forming an **estuary**. Here the fresh river water mixes with the salt water of the ocean forming **brackish** (slightly salty) water. The organisms that settle here need special adaptations for survival. They must be able to handle the increase or decrease in salt or to be able to migrate and leave the area as it changes. Many species of fish live in estuaries part of the time, but only a small percent have adapted to living there year-round. The largemouth bass is one freshwater fish that visits estuaries. The white perch is a fish that can live in the estuary without leaving. There are also saltwater visitors, such as the sandbar shark or flounder, that come during certain times of the year to live in estuaries.

Fish World: *Where Do Fish Swim? (cont.)*

Oceans

Most of the species of fish live in the world's oceans and seas. Three-fourths of the earth's surface is marine water. Just like the freshwater fish, saltwater fish are generally limited to certain areas of the ocean. Some fish prefer the surface water, while others like the middle areas best. A few prefer the depths of the ocean. The upper levels of the ocean consist of fish that like to live in large groups called **schools**, or shoals. The ocean is home to the weirdest of fish—**fishes of the abyss** (deep-ocean fish). These fish have enormous mouths filled with sharp teeth. Some have light organs distributed all over their bodies that produce a faint blue light. The tropical ocean is also home to two- and four-winged flying fish that make short gliding flights over the water. The wings are actually enlarged fins. The electric eel is another marine fish. It produces enough electricity to stun or kill its large prey. The ocean also houses the most colorful of fish. The tropical reefs provide camouflage and hiding places for these attractive fish. The level of the ocean and the temperature of the water play an important role in which fish live where. Shallow waters are home to fish like the hammerhead shark, flying fish, and manta ray. The continental shelf area is the preferred habitat of tuna, halibut, herring, and puffer fish. The continental slope is where cod, haddock, flounder, and swordfish live.

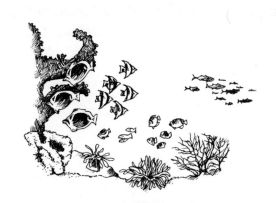

Some Common Freshwater, Saltwater, and Brackish Water Fish

Freshwater Fish	Saltwater Fish	Brackish Water Fish
Perch	Great White Shark	King Salmon
Paddlefish	Hagfish	Eel
Carp	Sea Trout	Bluefish
Brook Trout	Manta Ray	Shad
Gar	Lungfish	Lamprey
Pike	Toadfish	Atlantic Salmon
Crappie	Atlantic Flyingfish	
Bass	Whalefish	
Salmon	Seahorse	
Catfish	Weedy Seadragon	
Bluegill	Lion Fish	
Sunfish	Butterfly Fish	
Sturgeon	Swordfish	
Stickleback	Nile Mouthbrooder	
	Parrotfish	
	Marlin	
	Triggerfish	
	Barracuda	

Name:_____ Date: _____

Some Fish to Study: *Aquatic Research Project*

To the student observer: You're off to the library to learn which fish swims where. Fish swim in various aquatic habitats. Your teacher has assigned you a specific habitat. Research in the library or on the Internet to discover what kind of fish swim in your assigned habitat. Choose one species of fish for your research project. Gather information about your fish. Follow your teacher's directions for format and length of presentation. Your research should include the topics listed below.

Checklist for research topic

_____ 1. Fish name

_____ 2. Description of fish (what it looks like)

_____ 3. Drawing or photocopied picture (a visual aid—the Internet has nice images)

_____ 4. Size information (how big or small the fish is: length and weight)

_____ 5. Describe its habitat

_____ 6. Adaptations unique for your fish's survival (features that help it survive)

_____ 7. Behavior (your fish's habits or actions)

_____ 8. Two other facts about your fish that you discovered in your research

Extra Effort: Research to find the name of the largest fish. How large does it get, and where does it live? Write about it on your own paper.

* **Teacher Note:** This makes an excellent cooperative learning project. Make a bulletin board for freshwater, saltwater, and brackish water fish habitats. Display students' research in the classroom. Younger students may wish to record their research on the fish outline on the following page.

Name: _____ Date: _____

Some Fish to Study: *Aquatic Research Project (cont.)*

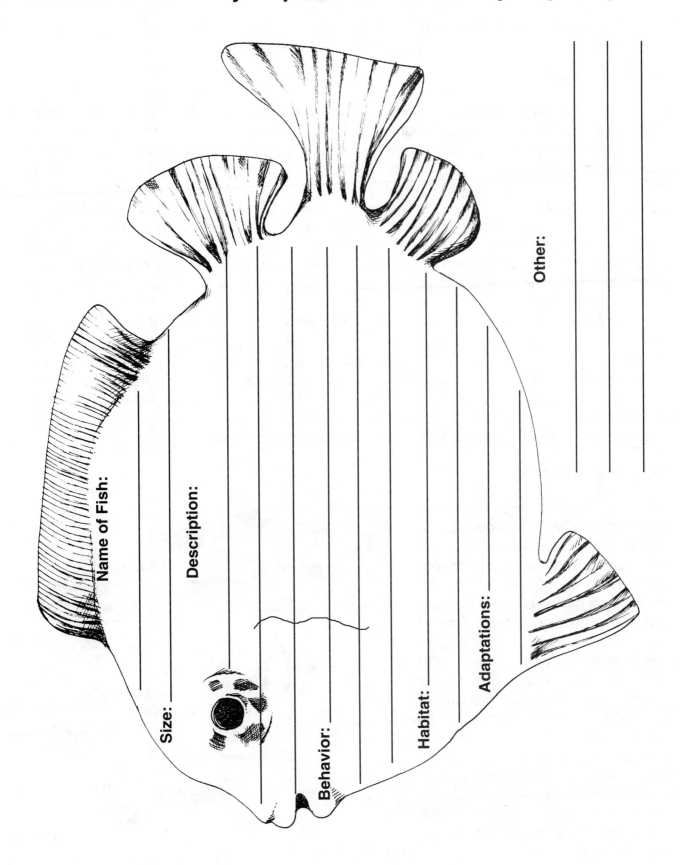

Other:

Name of Fish:

Description:

Size:

Behavior:

Habitat:

Adaptations:

Fish Reproduction: *Loads of Eggs*

Observers, have you ever had an opportunity to watch guppies or any other fish in a fish tank? Have you ever seen a guppy give birth or an angelfish lay eggs?

Fish Reproduction

Reproduction in most fish is a simple act. Most fish reproduce by external reproduction. **External reproduction** takes place outside the female's body. The female fish lays thousands of eggs called **roe** (ROH). The depositing of unfertilized eggs is called **spawning**. The male fish swims over the eggs and fertilizes them by releasing milt. **Milt** is a milky fluid that contains millions of free-swimming sperm. The sperm swim in the water until they reach an egg and fertilize it. The parents of most fish then leave the eggs on their own. Many **zygotes** (fertilized eggs) are formed. Each zygote divides many times, forming an **embryo** (developing fish). The embryo develops further into a very young fish called a **fry**. When the fry is fully developed, it hatches out of the egg. Each egg has its own food supply, which is the **yolk sac**. The yolk sac stays attached to the baby fish to provide **nourishment** (food) until the fish is big enough to search for its own food.

The fertilization of guppies takes place **internally** (inside the female's body). Guppies actually mate to produce offspring. The embryos develop internally also. The young guppies are born live. They are on their own from the time they are born. They swim off in search of food and to hide from danger. Some species of sharks are also an exception in fish reproduction. Some sharks release fertilized eggs in a long, hard case known as a **mermaid's purse**. The embryo develops inside the case. The black-tipped shark does not release fertilized eggs; the eggs remain inside the body until they have developed into fully-formed fry.

Temperature and Spawning

Fish lay many eggs so enough will survive to keep the species producing. Temperature is very important in the reproduction process. Each species has its favorite temperature for spawning. If the temperature isn't correct, spawning may not occur. Correct temperature also plays an important role in the development of the young fish. If it is too cold or too warm, the embryos do not develop properly or may even die. Each species has its own season and location in which it prefers to gather and spawn. Some fish prefer to spawn in shallow waters. Salmon make incredible journeys each year to spawn, returning to the same freshwater streams where they were hatched.

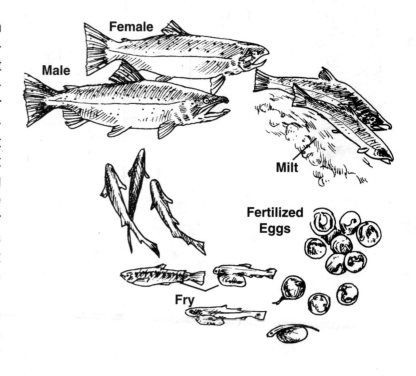

Female

Male

Milt

Fertilized Eggs

Fry

Name:_____ Date: _____

Fish Reproduction: *Reinforcement Activity*

To the student observer: Do you understand how fish reproduce? Explain the process.

_____

_____

_____

Analyze: If cod deposit between four and six million eggs at a single spawning, why aren't the world's oceans packed with codfish?

_____

_____

Directions: Answer the following questions.

1. What kind of reproduction is common to most fish? _____

    _____

2. What is the name given to a mass of fish eggs? _____

3. What is the depositing of unfertilized eggs by the female called? _____

4. What is the liquid the male releases over the roe called? _____

5. How does the sperm reach the eggs? _____

    _____

Directions: Complete the following sentences.

6. The fertilized egg is called a _____.

7. A(n) _____ forms after the zygote divides many times.

8. A very young fish is called a(n) _____.

9. The yolk sac's job is to _____ the fry.

10. _____ is very important for successful spawning.

11. _____ and _____ are both exceptions in fish reproduction; they reproduce by internal fertilization.

Unusual Breeders

Observers, some fish do not like to play by the rules. They are the exceptions to the reproduction and life cycles of most fish. Once the embryos develop, they usually hatch, leaving the egg stage behind them. The newly-hatched fry are now in the larva stage of development. The egg stage and larva stage each represent a very dangerous time in the life of a fish. If the fish manages to survive and not be eaten by other aquatic life, it is an amazing accomplishment. Let's take a look at some fish that dare to be different and follow their own rules for breeding.

Mouthbreeders

The mouthbreeders are a group of fish that seem to be careful parents. They carefully carry their fertilized eggs in their mouths until the young can cope with life. Since fish eggs are laid first and fertilized second, the task of incubating the eggs often falls to the males, since they were the last ones to see the eggs. To safeguard the hatch, the male tilapia scoops the eggs up into his mouth from the nest. It takes about five days for the eggs to hatch and another six to eight days for the young fish to complete development. Then they are spit out by the father. During this time, the father has refrained from eating or closing its jaw. Therefore, a young fry shouldn't swim back and forth in front of its hungry father too many times, or it may become swallowed by him. The female convoy fish carries her fertilized eggs in her mouth until they hatch. The larva then swim near their mother. In the event of danger, they dart back into her mouth for safety.

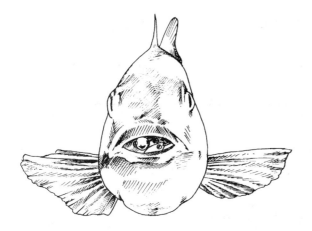

Female convoy fish: Fertilized eggs are kept in the mother's mouth until hatched. In the event of danger, they dart back into her mouth for safety.

Male tilapia: Eggs are kept in the father's mouth for safety until hatched. He then spits them out.

Unusual Breeders (cont.)

Pouchbreeders

Some fish carry their fertilized eggs in a pouch-like part of their bodies. The male seahorse, a fish that looks like a horse, lets the female seahorse lay her eggs in his brood pouch on his belly. The eggs develop in the male's pouch for two to six weeks until they are fully formed and ready to be born. The male grasps a piece of seaweed with his prehensile tail and then bends back and forth, opening the pouch. The baby seahorses shoot out of the pouch and rise to the surface to take gulps of air to fill their swim bladders.

Nesting

Birds aren't the only animals to build nests. The male brook stickleback builds a nest from aquatic plant material. He then chases several females into the nest, often hurrying them along by biting their tails. The females deposit their eggs and leave. The male remains behind to tend to the nest and guard the fry.

Fatal Breeding

Pacific salmon, born in freshwater streams, spend most of their lives in salt water. They too are unusual breeders. The salmon swim upstream for great distances to return to the same freshwater streams where they were hatched. The incredible journey has many obstacles to overcome, such as leaping over waterfalls. The salmon usually migrate to spawn only once; most of the salmon die shortly after spawning.

Name:_____ Date: _____

Unusual Breeders: *Reinforcement Activity*

To the student observer: Do you know any exceptions for fish reproduction? What are they?

_____

_____

_____

Analyze: How do these unusual breeders differ from most fish? _____

_____

_____

_____

Directions: Answer the questions below.

1. In what way are male seahorses different from most fish? _____

   _____

   _____

2. How does a young convoy fish avoid danger? _____

   _____

   _____

3. How are salmon different from most fish? _____

   _____

   _____

4. How are brook stickleback fish like birds? _____

   _____

   _____

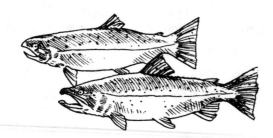

Fish Behavior: *The Art of Survival*

Fish, like all living things in the animal kingdom, have survival as their main objective. Obviously, fish have developed an effective means for survival. There are more fish than all the other vertebrates. One must ask how can this be with the complexities of reproduction? These amazing animals have developed adaptations that are unique to their survival. Fish display complex behaviors as they respond to their environment. Living things respond to stimuli in different ways. A **stimulus** is anything in the environment that causes a response. The way an organism responds to stimuli is called **behavior**. Behavior is the way an organism acts.

Protection and Scaring the Enemy

Fish must be ready to respond to predators; the underwater world is full of predators in search of prey. Size is one tactic; small fish need a burst of speed to quickly dart into small crevices. Large fish are often too large to swallow. **Camouflage** is another method of protection. Certain fish may have colors to match the shades and patterns of their surroundings, making it difficult for predators to see them. Some fish use their bright colors as a form of protection. Bright warning colors, such as red and white, alert other fish to stay away. Poisonous fish or nasty-tasting fish are usually brightly marked. Some fish, such as pufferfishes and porcupine fishes, protect themselves by **puffing up** (increasing their size) and sticking out their prickles or spines. Surgeonfish have a blade-like lancet that extends out on each side at right angles to the fish. These blades can be flicked out quickly and are as sharp as a surgeon's scalpel. Eyespots prove effective in defense tactics by giving the illusion of a big face. Both predator and prey use the landscape for hiding places. Predators hide and look for unsuspecting victims to swim by. In emergency situations, prey such as the twinspot wrasse hide in the sand or gravel by digging in and burying themselves. The filefish has a dorsal fin that locks upright and is used to help wedge it into small crevices. There are more than 50 kinds of poisonous fish that secrete a toxin or venom for defense. The lion fish is one of the most colorful and toxic fish in the sea. It has venomous spines all over its body. Some fish find shelter by hiding among the poisonous tentacles of other animals. A few fish, such as the electric eel, generate their own electric shock for protection.

Incredible Voyages and Social Behaviors

Scientists have observed that fish demonstrate many social behaviors. Fish may live in groups or alone. About one-fourth of all fish live in schools all their lives. About half the fish live in schools when they are young. **Schools** are large groups of individual fish that live close together. Schools move in ribbon-like, spherical, iceberg-shaped, or irregular formations. The number of fish and size of the fish seem to limit the school. Fish swim together for protection. A large school may help fool a predator into thinking the school is one huge fish. When facing danger, some schools scatter and flee while others move closer together.

Fish migrate to reach breeding grounds and pursue food and favorable water temperatures. Journeys may be made daily or once in a lifetime. If the fish cannot adapt to the changes in their surroundings, they must leave in order to survive. Tuna, mackerel, salmon, and eel are all famous travelers.

Fish Behavior: *The Art of Survival (cont.)*

Forming Relationships

Fish develop relationships within their environment. The most common relationship is that of **predator and prey**. This relationship helps to maintain the balance in nature. In this relationship, the **predator** (hunter) benefits by surviving while the **prey** (hunted) dies. Another relationship called **mutualism** is when both species benefit from the relationship. The cleaner fish feeds on the dead skin and parasites that live on another fish. The cleaner gets room and board while the other fish is thoroughly cleaned of parasites and dead skin. Little fish called remora eat tiny parasites that grow on a shark's skin. The relationship of **parasitism** exists when one species benefits, and the other is harmed. The lamprey feeding on a bony fish is an example of parasitism. The lamprey benefits, while the bony fish (the host) is eventually harmed. **Commensalism** is a relationship in which one species benefits from the relationship while the other species isn't affected. They do not gain or lose anything in the relationship. The pilot fish and a shark make an excellent example of commensalism. The pilot fish swims close to the shark waiting for the shark to feed. As the shark feeds, the pilot fish cleans up all the scraps of food that float away from the shark's mouth. The pilot fish benefits while the shark isn't affected in any way.

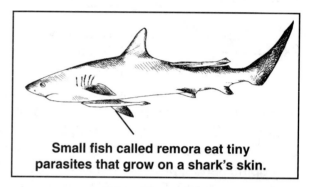

Small fish called remora eat tiny parasites that grow on a shark's skin.

Keeping Mankind in Line

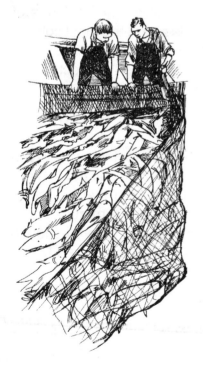

One serious survival factor facing fish and their future is mankind. Mankind throughout the world depends on fish for a source of protein. This may result in the overfishing of many species of fish. Migrating and schooling fish are easy and predictable targets for the fishing industry. If we continue to overfish the oceans, we will lose some of the species we have become dependent on. We must reach international agreement on how many fish can safely be taken.

Overfishing is just one way man has proven to be an enemy of fish. We also pollute their waters by dumping chemicals and waste in them. We destroy their habitats where they feed and spawn. We even bring new predators to the waters by introducing non-native fish to the ecosystem. Often the non-native fish adapt very well and compete for food and nesting sites, threatening the existence of the native fish. We must all work together to decrease the number of unnatural factors introduced by mankind that affect the fish in our world.

Name:_____ Date: _____

Fish Behavior: *Reinforcement Activity*

To the student observer: Do you know some ways mankind has become an enemy to fish?

_____

_____

Analyze: In your opinion, which of the defensive behaviors of schools of fish is the most beneficial and why?

_____

_____

Directions: Answer the following questions.

1. What is a stimulus? Give an example of a stimulus in your environment. _____

    _____

    _____

2. What is behavior? _____

    _____

3. What are some of the ways fish protect themselves? _____

    _____

    _____

4. What is warning coloration, and how is it helpful? _____

    _____

    _____

5. What are schools of fish, and how is this a helpful behavior? _____

    _____

    _____

6. How do schools of fish react to danger? _____

    _____

7. Describe the four relationships fish develop in their environments.

    a. _____

    b. _____

    c. _____

    d. _____

Name:_____ Date: _____

Fish Vocabulary: *Study Sheet*

To the student observer: This is a list of important terms used throughout the unit. Use this sheet to help you do the activities in the fishes unit. You can also use this list of terms to help you study for the Unit Test.

1. **Agnatha -** Class name for jawless fish

2. **Camouflage -** Protective coloration (blending in with surroundings)

3. **Chondrichthyes -** Class name for cartilaginous fish

4. **Chordate -** An organism that has a notochord, gill slits, and a hollow nerve cord

5. **Classification -** To group organisms according to similar traits

6. **Cold-blooded -** Body temperature changes with its surroundings

7. **Dichotomous key -** Used to identify organisms

8. **Ectotherm -** An animal that is cold-blooded

9. **Embryo -** A developing zygote (fertilized egg)

10. **Fins -** Structures used by fish for movement

11. **Fry -** A young fish (larva stage)

12. **Gills -** Structures used by fish for breathing

13. **Ichthyology -** The study of fish

14. **Lateral line system -** A sensory organ that detects movement in water

15. **Osteichthyes -** Class name for bony fish

16. **Scales -** The protective body covering of fish

17. **Spawning -** The act of fish laying large numbers of eggs

18. **Swim bladder -** A sac that inflates with gases (helps fish float)

19. **Vertebrates -** Animals who have an internal skeleton with a backbone

20. **Yolk sac -** Food source for embryos

Name:_____ Date: _____

Fishes: *Crossword Puzzle*

To the student observer: Use the information you have learned during your fish unit to complete the puzzle below.

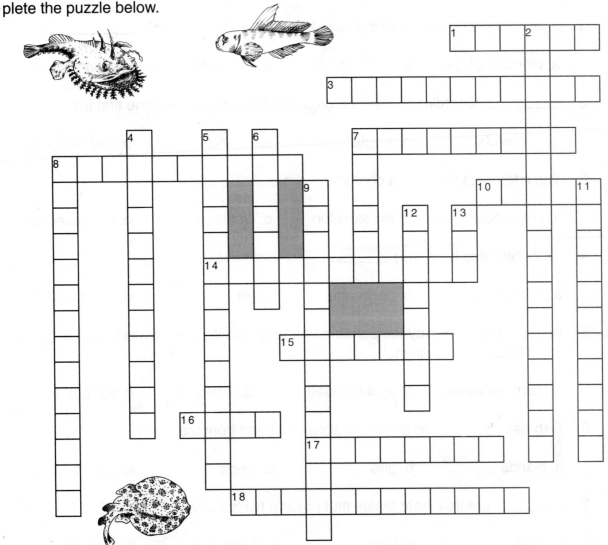

ACROSS

1. Protective body coverings
3. Animals who have an internal skeleton with a backbone
7. An animal that is cold-blooded
8. Protective coloration (blending in with surroundings)
10. Structures used by fish for breathing
14. The study of fish
15. Food source for embryos (two words)
16. Structures used by fish for movement
17. The act of fish laying large numbers of unfertilized eggs
18. Class name for bony fish

DOWN

2. A sensory organ used by fish to detect movement in water (three words)
4. Body temperature changes with the surroundings (hyphenated word)
5. Grouping organisms according to similar traits
6. Class name for jawless fish
7. A developing zygote
8. Class name for cartilaginous fish
9. Used to identify organisms (two words)
11. A sac that inflates with gases (helps fish float) (two words)
12. An organism that has a notochord, gill slits, and hollow nerve cord
13. A young fish (larva stage)

Name:_____ Date: _____

Fishes: *Unit Test*

Directions: Place the letter of the term that best completes each sentence on the line.

_____ 1. A person who studies and monitors fish populations is a (an) _____.

        a. biochemist   b. ichthyologist   c. paleontologist   d. environmentalist

_____ 2. _____, according to fossil records, are considered to be the first fish.

        a. Lancelets   b. Hagfish   c. Sharks   d. Ostracoderms

_____ 3. The internal skeleton of a chordate is the _____.

        a. nerve cord   b. exoskeleton   c. cartilage   d. endoskeleton

_____ 4. All vertebrates have a(n) _____.

        a. exoskeleton   b. backbone   c. gill   d. swim bladder

_____ 5. An animal whose body temperature changes with the temperature of its surroundings is a _____ animal.

        a. warm-blooded   b. cold-blooded   c. chordate   d. vertebrate

_____ 6. Fish use _____ to absorb dissolved oxygen from the water.

        a. glands   b. gills   c. lungs   d. scales

_____ 7. _____ are thin, hard plates that cover a fish's body.

        a. Scales   b. Fins   c. Tunicates   d. Shields

_____ 8. _____ are fanlike structures for steering and balance.

        a. Scales   b. Fins   c. Operculums   d. Chordates

_____ 9. The flexible tissue that is not as hard as bone is called _____.

        a. cartilage   b. notochord   c. endoskeleton   d. ligaments

_____ 10. Of the following, the trait that is not a characteristic of all chordates is _____.

        a. gill slits   b. notochord   c. hollow nerve cord   d. fins

Name:_____ Date: _____

Fishes: *Unit Test (cont.)*

_____ 11. There are more species of _____ than all the other vertebrates.

   a. amphibians   b. mammals   c. fish   d. sharks

_____ 12. _____ use their mouths to attach to fish by suction.

   a. Lampreys   b. Tunicates   c. Skates   d. Rays

_____ 13. Of the following, the example that is not a class of fish is the _____.

   a. jawless fish   b. jawed fish   c. cartilaginous fish d. bony fish

_____ 14. Most fish float because they have a _____.

   a. pectoral fin   b. swim bladder   c. buoyancy gland d. lateral line

_____ 15. _____ do not have swim bladders.

   a. Hagfish   b. Seahorses   c. Sharks   d. Catfish

_____ 16. Fish use a sensory organ called the _____ to detect movement in water.

   a. swim bladder   b. brain   c. spawning   d. lateral line

_____ 17. To group organisms according to their similar traits is called _____.

   a. chondrichthyes   b. classification   c. dichotomous key d. osteichthyes

_____ 18. The largest and most varied group of fish is the _____.

   a. bony fish   b. cartilaginous fish c. jawless fish   d. jawed fish

_____ 19. The science of classification is called _____.

   a. organization   b. ichthyology   c. taxonomy   d. biology

_____ 20. The smallest and oldest group of fish is the _____.

   a. bony fish   b. cartilaginous fish c. jawless fish   d. jawed fish

Answer Keys

What Is a Fish?: Reinforcement (p. 3)
Observer: Gills
Analyze: The body temperature would drop.
1. simplest
2. ectothermic
3. changes
4. Any order:
   a. ectothermic
   b. have scales
   c. swim with fins
   d. breathe with gills
5. Any order:
   a. Agnatha—jawless fish
   b. Chondrichthyes—cartilaginous fish
   c. Osteichthyes—bony fish

What Are Vertebrates?: Reinforcement (p. 5)
Observer: The brain
Analyze: The digestive system
1. Any order:
   a. notochord
   b. gill slits
   c. hollow nerve cord
2. Any order:
   a. invertebrate: animals without backbones or internal skeletons
   b. vertebrates: animals with backbones or spines; they have internal skeletons
3. Any order:
   a. ectothermic: cold-blooded animals; the surroundings regulate their body temperature
   b. endothermic: warm-blooded animals; they maintain a constant body temperature

Vertebrates: Crossword Puzzle (p. 6)

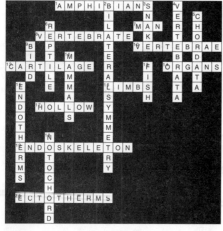

Observers: All have a backbone inside their bodies. (All have an internal skeleton.)

The History of Fish: Reinforcement (p. 9)
Observer: The ostracoderm
Analyze: This allows for a more varied diet and increases the food sources available.
1. fins, scales, and movable jaws
2. They study fossils.
3. The coelacanth is called a living fossil because scientists thought it was extinct. It looks just like the ancient fossils.
4. a. 1
   b. 7
   c. 2
   d. 5
   e. 3
   f. 4
   g. 6

External Anatomy: Reinforcement (p. 11)
Observer: Fish have streamlined shapes and compact bodies with narrow, pointed snouts. They are covered with a lubricating mucous. Their fins propel them through the water and stabilize them.
Analyze: Its body is streamlined and compact. It has a narrow snout that helps it cut through the water.
1. Any order:
   a. caudal: propels fish forward
   b. dorsal and anal: stabilizers; keep them from rolling over
   c. pelvic: maneuvering and braking
   d. pectoral: maneuvering and braking
2. Any order:
   a. cycloid: carp and salmon (bony fish)
   b. ctenoid: bass, bluegill, and perch (bony fish)
   c. placoid: sharks and rays (cartilaginous fish)
   d. ganoid: gar (primitive fish)
3. protection
4. a. ganoid
   b. ctenoid
   c. cycloid
   d. placoid

Internal Anatomy: Reinforcement (p. 13)
Observer: Fish have swim bladders that allow them to adjust their buoyancies. They breathe through gills, which obtain oxygen from the water. They have a lateral line system that allows them to detect movement in the water. They also have a keen sense of smell.
Analyze: Accept any logical answers.
1. They inflate or deflate their swim bladders to raise or lower themselves.
2. They do not have swim bladders.

3. Sharks
4. It is a sensory organ that helps fish detect water movement or currents. (It is a canal connected to sensory nerves scattered over the skin.)
5. They receive a constant supply of oxygen as the water flows over their gills.
6. The other senses are extremely developed and much more important for survival in water.

Internal and External Anatomy: Reinforcement (p. 14)

1A. snout
C. brain
E. pelvic fin
G. gills
I. lateral line
B. operculum
D. dorsal fins
F. caudal fin
H. swim bladder
J. scales
2. The gills
3. They help the fish move through the water.
4. Breathing
5. Sensing movement and water currents. (It helps guide them in the water.)
6. The swim bladder

Classification: Reinforcement (p. 16)

1. human
3. human
5. human
7. fish
9. human
11. fish
13. Yes
15. No, they each have individual traits.
2. fish
4. human
6. fish
8. fish
10. human
12. fish
14. group

Fish World Diversity: Reinforcement (p. 21)
Observers: In the oceans
Analyze: Lakes and ponds are home to many bony fish. These environments change drastically in comparison to the oceans. The fish have to adapt to these changes, or they would die.
1. a. jawless fish: hagfish and lamprey
   b. cartilaginous fish: sharks, rays, and skates
   c. bony fish: answers will vary
2. Agnatha is the oldest and simplest class. They are jawless, have no scales or paired fins, have cartilaginous skeletons, and live as parasites and scavengers.
3. Osteichthyes is the largest class. They have hinged jaws, scales, paired fins, lateral line systems, covered gills, swim bladders, and bony skeletons.
4. Chondrichthyes
5. The jawless fish, Agnatha

Name That Shark!: Classification Activity (p. 22)
1. Animalia
2. Chondrichthyes

3. Chordata
4. Sphyrnidae
5. *Sphyrna lewini*
6. Latin
7. There are often too many common names; it avoids errors in communication.
8. Carolus Linnaeus

Identifying Shark Families: Using a Dichotomous Key (p. 25)

A. Dasyatidae
C. Scapanorhynchidae
E. Hexanchidae
G. Pristiophoridae
I. Isuridae
K. Rhincodontidae
B. Sphyrnidae
D. Pseudotriakidae
F. Mobulidae
H. Rajidae
J. Alopiidae
L. Scyliorhinidae

Simulating Buoyancy: Student Lab (p. 26–27)
Observations:
1. The balloon should float up quickly to the surface.
2. The balloon should float only part way up to the surface.
3. Each time more air is added, the balloon should rise and float higher. (At a point, it will surface as fully inflated.)

Results and Conclusions:
1. The more air in the balloon, the more able it is to float.
2. The swim bladder is below the backbone in the middle of a fish. It is larger than the other organs.
3. It gets bigger. It makes the fish lighter, and its body expands. The fish floats upward.
4. It gets smaller. It makes the fish heavier. The fish sinks.
5. The gases are dissolved into the bloodstream from water that passes through the gills.
6. The balloon represents the swim bladder. The keys represent the weight or mass of the fish.
7. The fish can fill or empty its swim bladder to achieve different levels in the water.

Fish Reproduction: Reinforcement (p. 33)
Observers: The female fish deposits unfertilized eggs (spawning), and the male fertilizes the eggs by releasing milt over them. The free-swimming sperm fertilize the eggs. The fertilized eggs (zygotes) develop into embryos and then fry. The fry hatches from the egg and is fed by the yolk sac for a time.
Analyze: Most of the eggs do not survive to develop into fish.
1. external reproduction
2. roe
3. spawning
4. milt
5. They are free-swimming. They swim to the egg.

6. zygote
7. embryo
8. fry
9. feed
10. Temperature
11. Guppies, sharks

Unusual Breeders: Reinforcement (p. 36)
Observer: Answers will vary: seahorses, convoy fish, salmon, tilapia, brook stickleback
Analyze: They tend to their eggs and brood.
1. They carry their fertilized eggs in a pouch until they are fully developed.
2. They swim into their mother's mouth for safety.
3. They migrate upstream to spawn only once, and then die shortly after spawning.
4. They both lay eggs in a nest.

Fish Behavior: Reinforcement (p. 39)
Observer: Overfishing, pollution, destruction of habitat, introduction of non-native fish
Analyze: Answers will vary: Scatter—the predator can't catch all of them. Move closer together—the predator can't single out any one of them.
1. A stimulus is anything in the environment that causes a response. Examples will vary.
2. Behavior is the way an organism acts or responds to stimuli.
3. Hiding, toxins, electric shock, warning coloration, camouflage, using sharp spines or fins, puffing up, etc.
4. When the fish uses bright colors, such as red and white, it warns others that it is poisonous or nasty-tasting; it makes predators beware.
5. Schools are large groups of individual fish living and moving close together in formation. Schools may confuse predators and keep the members safe.

6. The individual fish may scatter, or they may move closer together.
7. a.   predator/prey: One, the predator, gains something (food); the other, the prey, loses and becomes a victim.
   b.   mutualism: Both gain something from the relationship.
   c.   parasitism: The host provides something for the predator; one is helped, and the other is harmed.
   d.   commensalism: One species is helped while the other is not affected.

Fishes: Crossword Puzzle (p. 41)

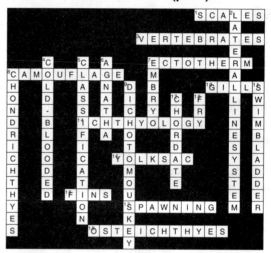

Fishes: Unit Test (p. 42–43)

1. b	2. d	3. d	4. b
5. b	6. b	7. a	8. b
9. a	10. d	11. c	12. a
13. b	14. b	15. c	16. d
17. b	18. a	19. c	20. c

Bibliography

Banister, Keith. *A Closer Look at Fish.* Gloucester Press, 1980.

Bernstein, Schachter, Winkler, and Wolfe. *Concepts and Challenges in Life Science.* Globe Fearon Inc., 1998.

Biggs, Daniel, and Ortleb. *Life Science.* Glencoe/McGraw-Hill, 1997.

Horton, Casey. *Fish.* Gloucester Press, 1985.

Ommanney, F. D. *The Fishes.* Time Life, Inc., 1969.

Parker, Steve. *Fish.* Eyewitness Books. Alfred A. Knopf, Inc., 1990.